The value of a sister
cannot be measured
but is always treasured.

To

from

6 Lamberti
6
2 Dupin
2 Federici
6 1 Topograph Cyprus
        Sconto 65
3 Alberti Dizion.
        Sconto
2 Zacharia
8 Berard
2 Ducci

30. —
3 Guarnieri
4 Norif
                8. —   24

L 30. L 90.
                5

Come si piague ordinario colla somma v. 15. 9bre
a mezzo del S.' Sebastiano Vergica di Pepra
contenendo tutti quegli ordini che i far posso
Commissione, egli altri mancai e che
spese e nostro assegno conce
Nella Spiaga di vedersi con più
ai quali fuspre proibci, con vera

Sconto 70
Sconto 45
Sconto 35

Thank You, Sister

new seasons™

Contributing writers: Rebecca Christian, Marie Jones,
Jennifer John Ouellette, Lynda Twardowski

Picture credits: © Corbis: Images.com; Robert McIntoch; Swim Ink.

New Seasons is a trademark of Publications International, Ltd.

Louis Weber, CEO
Publications International, Ltd.
7373 N. Cicero Avenue
Lincolnwood, Illinois 60712

www.pilbooks.com

Manufactured in China.

8 7 6 5 4 3 2 1

ISBN: 1-4127-0620-3

A friend may go the extra mile for you, but a sister will keep on going. Thank you for being there for me every step of the way.

I am blessed to have a sister who doesn't need to remind me who was born first or last, who is taller or prettier or more successful, who achieved this or won that. You have always let me be me, and you loved me for it no matter what.

Thank you for always making sure
I learned from your mistakes.

We're told when we are young to find someone to look up to—someone we'd like to imitate. I'm lucky. I didn't have to look far—I just looked to you.

For all the times you could have told on me and didn't—and for all the times you should have and did—thanks.

You've given me so much over the years, I'm not sure I know how I can ever repay you. Does the chicken pox I gave you when we were kids cover it?

We may not always see eye to eye, but we always feel heart to heart. Thank you for being the best sister in the world.

I've always been the envy of my friends for having such an amazing sister. Thank you for making me a legend in my own lifetime!

My right hand, my backbone,
my guts, my heart—you're not just
a part of my life, you're a part of me.

Thank you for always knowing exactly what to say, exactly when to say it, and exactly what kind of rich, gooey dessert to serve while saying it!

We always made the best sofa-cushion forts, created the most lifelike snowpeople, and designed the best sand castles. Thank you for helping to build my favorite childhood memories.

A sister's thoughtfulness is a gift like no other.
It is the only present that is offered solely out of love
and wrapped with absolutely no strings attached.

Thank you for being
the kind of sister
I can be proud of.

*I*f I am brave it's because
I know you would never
let me fight alone—
no matter how large or
small the obstacle.

People introduce us as sisters, but I know
we are so much more—trusted confidantes,
fine-tuned listeners, and expert advice
givers. Thank you for being my sister and so
much more.

When we were kids you always knew how to make me laugh. I'm so glad you still do.

Thank you for sharing my home, my history, my heart.

I am lucky to be your sister.
I am blessed to be your confidante.
I am honored to be your friend.

I'm so glad I have you to share things with— e-mails, phone calls, family stories, memories—even Dad's teasing and Mom's cooking!

You're saintly in your understanding. In one conversation with you, I can dump all my worries and concerns, and you simply carry them away with your angel wings.

I haven't always liked your advice, but I'm grateful you've loved me enough to give it.

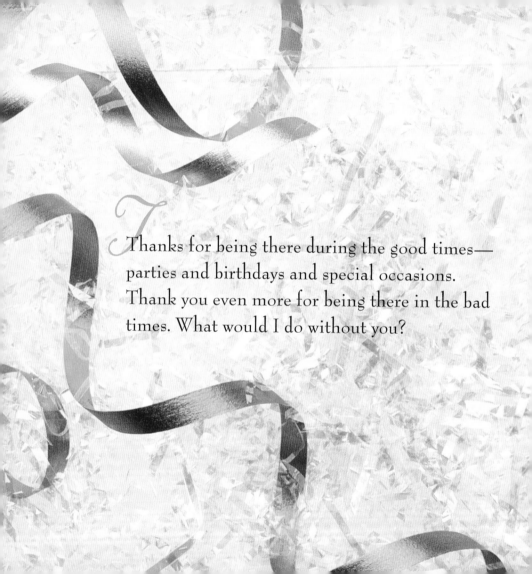

Thanks for being there during the good times—parties and birthdays and special occasions. Thank you even more for being there in the bad times. What would I do without you?

Mom always said one day we'd be grateful we had a sister. Guess she was right!

Thank you for never sharing the embarrassing secrets of my childhood, like the private concerts I performed in my bedroom with a hairbrush "microphone" or the ratty old teddy bear I couldn't sleep without.

The best support in life is not found in control-top pantyhose, shape-defining lingerie, or air-cushioned shoes. It's found in the caring words of a sister.

We were born to be sisters, but we were destined to become the best of friends. I thank the stars that you and I were meant to be.

Having you as a sister always made me try harder, reach higher, strive farther. Thank you for helping me become more than I ever could have alone.

Thank you for long talks
and even longer hugs.

You spice up every meal, liven up every dance, jazz up every song. What would I do without you?

Thanks for taking such good care of me. I know I was often a royal pain, but you never failed to treat me like a princess.

You never hesitate to give me unsolicited advice, tell me what you think is best for me, or offer me your opinion. And guess what? I wouldn't have it any other way. Thanks for caring so much.

To the only person who knows my true dress size—thanks. It's nice knowing my secrets are always safe with you.

Thanks, sis, for *always* being there for me, for *never* letting me down, and for even *sometimes* putting me in my place. I loved you then, and I cherish you now.

I never asked for a sister,
but I sure am thankful I got one.

I value every moment we've spent together—even the ones divided by an imaginary line down the middle of the backseat.

With us, there is no better or worse, greater or smaller, superior or inferior. You have always loved me and treated me as an equal, and for that I am grateful.

Thanks for never giving up on me.

Laughing at inside jokes, calling each other childhood nicknames, finishing each other's sentences—I'd rather share these things with you than anyone else in the world.

Because we are sisters, my life is so much more joyful.
Thank you for making every day brighter.

Sister, you've always been
my softest place to fall.

Thank you for getting into trouble first, making
mistakes first, and generally clearing the way for me.
You've made walking the path of life a whole lot easier!

Thank you for being my first roommate, my first playmate, and my first best friend.

Over the years, we've borrowed each other's clothing, lent each other money, given each other advice, and kept each other out of trouble. It's great having someone to share your life with!

Sent 25. July 2016

Sisters are forever, and I'm
forever glad you're mine.

Thank you, sister, for always being willing to lend me an ear and a shoulder to cry on. With you on my side, I feel like I can conquer the world.

Whenever I think about all the things
I am most grateful for in my life,
having you for my sister is right at
the top of my list.

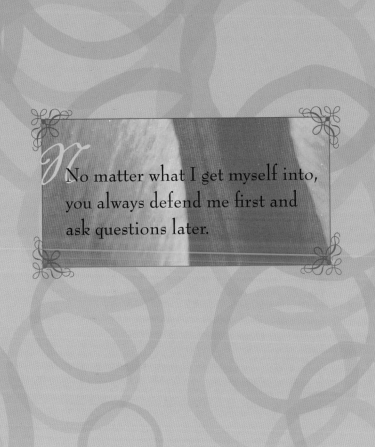

No matter what I get myself into,
you always defend me first and
ask questions later.

Thanks for being my lifelong pal.

If all the sisters in the world were lined up in a row—tall ones, short ones, smiling ones, serious ones, loud ones, quiet ones—I'd pick you.

Whether you're saving me from the monsters under my bed or the dark path I'm contemplating, you always reach out and pluck me from harm. Thanks for being my superhero.

Together, sis, we've weathered life's changing seasons and survived many turbulent storms. I can always count on you, my guiding light, my anchor, my safe and friendly shore.

You are the kind of sister every kid dreams of having and every adult hopes to grow old with.

Our relationship has been years of give and take. Thank you for always letting me *give* you all my problems so you could help *take* away my pain.

When we were little, I always felt better in any new or uncomfortable situation if you were around, too. Know what? I still do.

For all those times I took it for granted that you would lend me a buck, let me borrow your clothes, give me a ride, and not tell Mom and Dad (this time!), I'd like to say an enormous thank you now.

Sisters have a secret language all their own. It's like Morse code for the eyes—no words are ever needed. Thank you for always catching my drift.

When something good happened to me
when we were young, it never seemed quite
real to me until I could tell you all about it.
Come to think of it, I still feel that way.

Through laughter and tears,
events big and small,
relationships good and bad,
you've always been there for me.
Thanks.

Sister, you're an example worth living up to.

To the only person in my life who I can ask to inspect my teeth for spinach and my behind for a panty line—thank you.

I am so grateful for you, sister, and I wanted you to know what I often find so hard to put into words: You are my other half, my precious equal, my true and dearest friend.

Thanks for always sticking up for me.

Thank you for always being there to explain life's little mysteries: how to put on makeup, what to say to a guy, and why they sometimes never call again.

As a kid I admired everything you had. Now that we're grown, I admire everything you are.

I know you love me, but thanks for reminding me
all the time how much you do.

Sisters are supposed to fight, compete, and drive each other crazy, but not you. You rise above the rest; you're the cream of the crop, the best of the best.

You always knew just what to say to me and when to say nothing at all. Thank you for both.

Chance, not choice, made us sisters. But if I did have the choice, I would choose you again and again.

*I*t's probably impossible to thank your sister for all that she's taught you. But then again, when the best lesson she's shared is that nothing is impossible, it wouldn't be right not to try. So, thank you . . . a million times thank you.